THE LATE WORLD

ALSO BY ARTHUR SMITH

Orders of Affection
Elegy on Independence Day

THE LATE WORLD

poems by

Arthur Smith

Carnegie Mellon University Press
Pittsburgh 2002

ACKNOWLEDGMENTS

Grateful acknowledgment is made to the editors of the following publications in which these poems first appeared:

Atlanta Review ("Fog Sharks" under the title "Agents of Hunger, Agents of Fear"); *Chattahoochee Review* ("'Come Back, or Send Somebody'" and "Lines Written During a Recent 'Death of Poetry' Symposium"); *Crazyhorse* ("Pastoral" under the title "Heaven," "A Walk Late on the World's Fair Site," "Bad Dreams," "Roosters Every Morning," and "Absolute Grace in the Natural Order of Things"); *DoubleTake* ("Rome Was Made Possible by Such" and "More Lines on a Shield Abandoned During Battle"); *Gulf Coast* ("Cold Ode for the Starlings of Baltimore"); *The Kenyon Review* ("Lights from a Pier," "Roman Time," "Its Difficult Name," "At the Grave of an Ancient Poet," and "To an Early Greek Philosopher"); *The Nation* ("Hard Wood"); *Now and Then* ("The Brilliant Days"); *Prairie Schooner* ("Measure Being the Soul of Management"); *Shenandoah* ("Echo" and "Relativity").

"My Mother's Name in English" appeared originally in *The New Bread Loaf Anthology of Contemporary American Poetry*, eds. Michael Collier and Stanley Plumly, University Press of New England, 1999.

"With Marigolds" was first published in *This Much Earth*, eds. Christopher Buckley, David Oliveira, and Marty Williams, Heydey Press, 2000.

"Chez Lucille," "Good Deeds," and "The Rich Man Watches the Widower" were first published in *All Around Us: Poems from the Valley*, eds. Linda Parsons and Candace W. Reaves, Blue Ridge Publishing, 1996.

Thanks are due to the Department of English at the University of Tennessee for research leaves during which a number of these poems were written or begun. Special thanks to David Baker, David Kitchel, Julia Levine, Michael Nelson, Curt Rode, Grace Schulman, and Michael Starry.

The publication of this book is supported by a grant from the Pennsylvania Council on the Arts.

For Al Braselton,
"a friend to poets"

CONTENTS

I

II

III

"Jesus said,

'If the flesh came into being

because of spirit,

it is a wonder.

But if spirit came into being

because of the body,

it is a wonder

of wonders.'"

—*The Gospel of Thomas*

"COME BACK, OR SEND SOMEBODY"

Brush-painted as though yesterday
Red and wet and running

Down the whitewashed sheet of plywood,
Those letters have been alone

With the weather of northern Texas
For a long time, as has

The frame house they lean against,
Its porch- and floor-boards

Shot through
With a few weedy saplings.

For a moment, you might not know
If it were north or south

The bus headed, or why you were on it,
If one afternoon between Dallas and Waco you woke

And the first thing you saw was how little lasted,
And how long—

Though if you had been alone
With the weather anywhere

You'd know the house plowed
Newly up to and around,

And the scrub oaks bony in the wind,
And the way the wind points through them.

You'd know who left, and who stayed, and what happened next,
And why the bus drives on.

AT THE GRAVE OF AN ANCIENT POET

At the end of the line,
After the long walk
Over spring hills needled with a gray rain,
Here it is, as you said it would be,
A flat black stone floating
Over what remains—
Trees and rocks,
The stuff of my own life
Lightened
With your one buoy
To the living.

The woman I love has
Gone to hell,
And all I get is Zeno
Paralyzing
Death's approach with terminal thought,
And Pythagoras, Pythagoras
The only channel.

You were first
To learn what happened
After love, and after the love
Of death, and after death.

A man made brave
By love, this is
Your empty grave.

HARD WOOD

It must be oak, this simple device
I ease my back and the back
Of my head down onto
On the floor. Against it
The muscles fanning
My spine are pinched
In a pain more acute than
My own earlier over lunch
With a friend, when I was
Cruel to her wish
To discover the world
As she wished.
We argued, and I
Wound up with the ache
I'm laying out over this wooden bridge
Passed on
Friend to friend
By those who understand how
Thoroughly—sometimes—
The body needs to listen
To its own nerves
Cry against something—anything—
Until sound means nothing, and feeling nothing,
Until the sharp heart gives way to whatever's
Harder than the human head
And its unrelenting grain.

FIRST OF ALL

The urge has always
Been to offset the immediacy
Of the governing self,
Even as a child picnicking in a meadow
Lacquered by the late light of afternoon,
A night shore of cooled thicket shade and pine.

It must have been a moment
Overlooked by thought
When you glanced back, leaving,
And saw that green world
Crack, when the light behind it
Like a sparrow being freed

Flew *through*, and entered you.
Ever after, as you try to coax
That bright bird in again—or out—
It will look as though
You are spreading a blanket for two
And are sitting down alone.

TO GO THERE THIS MIND MUCH SINGS

In order to be with her, I used to fly in over
The plains nation of that endlessly central country—

Cattle ponds going from blue to blinding
In the clear second the sun crossed over—

High over live oaks, their leaf needles blurred—

Those mornings, those glories
Of light whisking
Wheat-colored over the table—
That roomful of bright warmth—

And now that it's gone—
How to return—

Not to the woman, not to the one
Only
A little while
Outlasting that fine life—

But to the one that burns within me all alone—

AT THE LARGE ANIMAL SANCTUARY

She likes
To do that, her keeper said.
She likes to
Smell your hair.

Like it or not,
I couldn't believe
I was kneeling in front of a 250 pound
Female Bengal tiger and letting her
Lick the crown of my head.

Extended slender
And still moist from her lungs,
Something like a tongue
Brushed at my scent
And drew me in.

I was no more myself then
Than I was anything else—

Sometimes the way
I'm the one writing the words,
Sometimes
The one leaning forward
To read.

CHEZ LUCILLE

The truth is, I'm wired
With you, music and talk
And me leaning

Close to your hair
And your face
And that sweet place

In back of your ear
Where the thin skin's
Drawn over bone.

I'm all right, I couldn't be
Drunk enough not
To want you,

Not be shown
How that long and low,
That slow-rising

Note is best
Teased out of you.
The truth is,

I'm here with you
Right now, and the jazz
Is loud, and it's late.

LIGHTS FROM A PIER

From here, I can see many things at night
Sitting out long enough
If I am willing to.
I can see all the way to heaven
And how indistinguishable it is
From the sea and its darkness
Except as the whitewash rubs
A little of it away.

I can see lights from the pier
Where the sinks are, for cleaning fish,
And a few ropes for tethering crab-traps,
Where I stood earlier
As the high-pitched children kicked
At the casual waves, and I can still see
The long white sleep-blown hair of the old
As they walked below me.

Merest of light on a sheen,
Just when I think there is nothing
Beyond you, from behind me I hear a sound
Something like my love brushing her hair
She washed the sea from
Only minutes earlier,
The sea winds whipping a bit,
Helping to dry and make it shine.

MY MOTHER'S NAME IN ENGLISH

My mother going
Back door to front
Shadows a frailty
All the way from
Her kitchen to
This small wooden
Desk I'm watching
Her from tonight.

Back door to front,
The two portals
Swinging on darkness,
Swinging on light,
The winter-insistent
Bermuda not even
Knitted back through
Her daughter's grave.

Wiping her hands,
Back door to front,
Pursuing a note
No one can hear,
Though her name
In English means
"Iris," though
She is not brave.

She would rather
Not go back
Door to front,

From before knowing
Begins, to after
Knowing matters,
Over and over
Everything between.

I can't even
Call it brutal—
Not with everything
Between—my mother
Going back
Door to front,
And no one at either,
No one at either.

NIGHT LIGHT

It's like
Going to bed at night—you can't
Help it—when someone you love dies,
You go there, too.

You try to imagine sitting
Curled up forever
In a space so lightless your hands
Cannot be seen—

Then, after a while, without trying,
You can make out one
Dim fire like a star
Very far away.

So, there you are.

Now you can't sleep
With that light on.

COLD ODE FOR THE STARLINGS OF BALTIMORE

Once, in a December
Bitter even for Baltimore,
I paced all of one sun-blinding glassy afternoon
Into a place I haven't yet found
My way out of.

I had been sweating it out
In one of those high-rise rooms
Sealed off from the Chesapeake
And from the one step
Separating me
From two men far down below.

They were turning down cardboard
Like bedcovers
The same stiff color
As their overcoats,
And easing down and leaning back,
Their feet banked in the hiss of the sun
Off the bright ice of the building.

As they talked, their voices
Whitened and flattered
Whatever warmth they issued
Back out into the coldest of cloudless skies,
And I couldn't stop thinking of them
Pillowing their heads
On the same cold steps
Poe might have closed his eyes forever on.

All I can see now, thinking of this,
Is dusk heaping up
Whatever dust it can.

—And now God's ugly, that starling, on the ledge again.

I had forgotten
The two birds we were
That whole time spent together separately,
The starling huffing up against the heated glass
While I walked
From the door to the window sheers,
To the windowpane,
To the ledge—
My whole life down
To a leathery bird and a drunk dead.

One can't stay.

The other won't leave.

ROME WAS MADE POSSIBLE BY SUCH

He was so pleadingly out of his mind with her
On the phone that morning he almost missed it,

So deftly and sweetly she delivered the blow.
She must have sensed the moment he lifted

His foot and was talking bent over trying to stem
The bleeding of a toe he'd caught on something

Just when her ringing claimed him. She saw
Him in the kitchen, the sunlight green-tinted

And scented with basil on the sill, bookcases
Showering vines tangled with emerald leaves,

And cuttings in jars, their gill-like white roots
Seining it in, the new world. As long

As she could, she held and calmed
His mind in her lap, that room bright and full.

And then, as gently as she had to, she turned
His mind against her until she made it stop.

THE RICH MAN WATCHES THE WIDOWER

He needs to touch her things,
The paper bags and ribbons,
The buttons and thread and small
Round silver pellets

That look like dainty rivets—
Though what a woman would need
Rivets for
Escapes him.

These are the others
Others leave behind,
And he is,
From now on,

Not without being
Puzzled by them,
From now on never
Not shining them with his fingers

When he's standing still,
Never not hearing
Their currency
When he walks.

ROMAN TIME

Of course I can't sleep at night.
Of course I have
Bad dreams.

Memory is some cold
Woman I thought of once
Standing in the shallows
Of a waste pond
Filthier
Than the rags she was trying to beat clean.

Now I find her on the terrace—
Up late, like me—
Measuring and mending, attending
To that slowest of beliefs—that the slower even
Balance the world works
Makes God
God,
And God the world, and God
Breathing us
In the chill shallows of the night,
And our whispering back out
That silvery presence.

Nothing else keeps me out under
As many shattered stars
As I can hope only
To see again,
With not one among them
Bearing
One of us witness.

This is the coldest I've ever been.

How long have we been
Out here?

ECHO

All right, I'll meet you
For a walk
On the late world's fair site—

Or on Pontchartrain, if the choppy
City side of the causeway
Agrees with you.

—Or at Ella's or Lucille's, where you might be singing
Under someone else's name.

I'm less willing
To believe
We'll meet again,
Though I find myself all the more hungering
That wonder of bewilderment
In the wakened fable of
What happened.

But after all this time—
After the spirit's been broken
And its flesh revealed—

Finding myself
Out here alone again, depending

On a medium no less likely
Than water or flesh or faith
Being firm—I can't believe it—
The wind rising—and the waves—

BAD DREAMS

They must come closer
To morning than evening—stars and moons,

The distantly enormous gathering

A view through the high window
Several tones
Lighter than the room.

When I look back, I can't
Help but think
It's a blessing,

Seeing her blonde and tawny again—
The hillside behind her swaying with poppies—

And all of them strained from the earth,
And all of them thriving
In the low chill wind.

It makes me think if I were
Out there, I would make
As many breaths as I could make
Partial under a December sky.

It makes me think if I were
Farther away, somewhere
I've never been, and were walking
The long way home, I might know
Happiness in its moment—

Mountains of sunlight, pillars of rain.

MEASURE BEING THE SOUL OF MANAGEMENT

For a death more fathomless than I can
Imagine, and for the emptiness ever after—

For the nights, too, awful
When my only heart was company, both of us

Breathless until the darkness billowing
At the window gave way

To the morning's calm lustreless upon me—
And for the day's allowance

Against which all things must now be measured—
Especially the silences which will not leave me

Alone—
          and for the rudeness of memory
Which will not leave me alone among them—

PASTORAL

He can't believe
It's three in the morning
Into Sunday's dark apartments—
From overhead comes
Bounding down
Some sort of music
Irrelevant as revenge.

The gift of a breeze ruffles
Summer from a balcony
The same seductive
Hue in a streetlamp's murk
As wisteria clustering
Its Concords
Swollen by moonlight.

That's when the steel
Horn of a pick-up
Pitches
Its long way winding
Up the drive,
The held blare trolling
The parked cars—

Two girls from
The waist up bare
In the truck bed singing,
And whooping it up,
And waving like
Sparklers
Their white tops.

WITH MARIGOLDS

Knowing you sometimes is like
Just now—
An afternoon shower thinning to mist,
The shale-colored cloud veneer
Here and there pin-holed with light.
Out and in, the dogs bounding
Down and up again
The steps
Into the yard. I let them
Out,
And into the weather
Of that grayness a neighbor's marigold opened
Its hundred of bunches of hands
And the sun's fire filled them at the same instant
I happened to look. It was
There all along,
That wild paradise
Of being lost
And being found.

ROOSTERS EVERY MORNING

Okay, so maybe you don't believe
A man and woman
Could live as she and I did,

And burn like that,
And live.

And it seems you're right.

This morning I'm up
And at it again, dressing,
And eating, and knowing less and less—

Still eager
For your lure when spring beams from the cowbird-peppered
                                        poplars—

Or from the screech violin of standing up my knees—

Or from two books set out on a table
Like gloves and their warning—

My cold star,
Mutuality,

I'm with you—

I'm up—

TELL ME AGAIN

Each time, I find you
        somewhere else, this time
                backstage, carnival, hand-feeding

Acorns to the black bears
        no one else could master.
                Just in time, you're starting up

The oldest story anyone remembers—
        two lovers, and the haven they found
                ticking between them—

What I keep forgetting
        is how, by story's end, you have
                all of us smiling—you and me,

The fed bears, the broken lovers—
        each time, we can see the story
                is going to end with us—

GOOD DEEDS

It's easy to forget the bathtub
I'm scrubbing is the same one
She once drew hot water in

And undressed me for
And into which I pooled myself
After a long, down day's work.

Sometimes when I think of her, I remember
A woman asking the man she loved
If he thought

She were beautiful—the man
Saying nothing, believing she were the one
Tried by that question.

A good number of down days would pass
Before his knowing
The difference, before his saying

She was beautiful, to himself aloud,
And again, for good measure,
To the tub.

SONNET

Once, turning her over, he happened, glancing,
To see hooves, two hooves on the sheets

Where his feet should have splayed.
Under him, her head lolling,

She was so far gone within
He could know that place only by the sounds she uttered
       entering it.

Mythic bliss, he had boasted.
Later, he wasn't sure.

What did the hooves mean?
And why had he felt such awe in her pleasure, and such pleasure
       in his work, in driving

The woman there
Though he couldn't stay?

—And what did
The hooves mean?

HOUSE DRINKS

If this is one of those stories
They try to soothe you with
When all you have left are the sharp hills
Trouble's backed you up against,

Save it.
I'll tell you something
Colder than the real hills—being blind.
And worse than that—being

Blind.
If we can agree on the ice in our drinks
Melting as we speak,
Sooner than your own mind

You can change that.
Sooner
Than your own mind, you can change weathers
And see an avenue so brightly rinsed

You have to
Close your eyes.
Sooner than your own mind,
Up springs the umbrella,

And you shiver.

TWICE REMOVED

It's difficult to say
What happened,
Except by saying
Every day she worked
He locked the loft behind him
And walked until he found himself in the park.

Under elms scattering some
Of the oldest leafing in North America, he sat on benches
In sunlight and shade, in light mist, in fog,
Or he rested on the tough spring grasses
Or on the humped-up roots of trees
Long polished by the weather of constant children.

He liked closing his eyes
With the season's heat,
And he liked the leaves shadowing the disappearing elms,
And especially he liked the way those shapes
Always made him think
Of Portland.

He could make out
In that city of a leaf's shadow
The Willamette towing its gray slag
To the Pacific's cauldron,
And Mount Hood's white bell rung by the sun
Sometimes briefly on its back.

He could see highways,
And alleyways with dumpsters,
And sidewalks after the lunch hour.
He could see a man slowing a door closing behind him,
        and hesitating.
He could see a woman passing in front of him, likewise
Lost in thought.

ABSOLUTE GRACE IN THE NATURAL ORDER OF THINGS

The finest thing one woman
He ever got tangled up with
Left behind
Was a headstrong mongrel of a fixed bitch

As fierce-looking as a Doberman
The size of a Pekinese.
Days long in the wake she trailed
Became

Mere days again,
And during them, there were plenty
Of times of plenty
He gleaned

From a hand-down dog something
Of a sense of humor, the sense
For looking on
The brighter side of things.

He liked to think he had
The best she had
To give
Until it died.

SATURDAY NIGHT/SUNDAY MORNING

I'm showering
Down
This body of a breath
My father and mother once
Misted between them,
Both of their faces
Blinded, no doubt,
By starlight and Pennsylvania
Coal dust.

I can smell yesterday's oils,
The skin's soiled silks,
And the sweet inner
Corolla
Of a woman's musk
Lowered several notes
By the small particles
Of cigarette smoke
Stuck to the bent hairs
Of my beard
Since last night's carousing
Being rinsed away.

And, yes, I can hear
You, too, as though
From the doorway
Of an adjoining room,
Some part of my mind
Going on,

Always going on
About *could have* and *should,*
And always during the *here*
And *now,* when
I'm trying to make
Way for the day.

MORE LINES ON A SHIELD ABANDONED
DURING BATTLE

The one time I said something
Awful to someone
I didn't know the meaning of,
It hardly mattered to him how empty
My head was
As his three younger brothers jumped
Down from the barn loft they slept in
And closed ranks behind him.

The hen he'd been about to kill
Rejoined a few others feeding
Near the stump.

—Are you talking to me? he said.

And it's true—
As you and anyone who's ever scattered knows,
And usually sooner—someone or something
Will ask what you mean—
The quicker
The world lives in a person,
The earlier he learns
To ask.

I'm trying
To imagine racing over
Someone's countryside, and making off with its riches—
As you and your brief nation did—
Then coming up
Face to face
With one of them better armed.

I'm glad we ran, both of us, having
Straddled that line
Beyond which
There are only dogs' jaws
Candid
About the river of death,
And how there are no limits to its length,
And how someone had better live
To tell the others.

TO AN EARLY GREEK PHILOSOPHER

It was a black day when whoever it was
After you, Thales, potted the first
Scrawny doubt of a cypress that towers now into the clouds
Over the west coast of the millennium
I live in.
I can almost believe
He meant no harm.
I can almost
Pity him
For having forever to pick
At the unlocked lock of the absurd
And for having to prove the zero
Ideas can lead to.

But how can you pity
A whistle at your back,
Wind
Through a root system forever
About to flower?

How can you pity the unborn, Thales,
Those cypresses of thought?

There have been days
I've heard that winded
Surge,
Ancient and noteless,
That music you gave thought to,
The sound of your own heart
As though it were the heart of someone
Who might be me, now,
Overlooking a prospect
Unendingly
Blue.

EASTER

Early April, there are still
Mindfuls of furred snow
Smudged in the gutters,
Like dough that gums up

Corners of the bread pan
When the soft hot loaf's
Rocked out
And you look inside.

It's like that every spring—

The sheer dumb thrust of it—
The earnestly uttered
One-toned notes,
The color-criers and the wet spikes

Bright with the green
Blood of God
Driven through from the other world—
Every winter of a day I forget,

O first of all—

RELATIVITY

Stein's so Zen. By Stein, I mean
My wife beautiful Mary's Keeshond—
Fifty pounds of charcoal hair
Streaked where it billows
A white halo around his head.

On a chokechain we go down sparkling
Over an afternoon's hill just before Halloween
At the end of a century closing a millennium.

To the curb he lurches, to the pines
Over long weeds tethered to the sun, and in constant blur
I'm trying not to
Step in it again.

By it, I mean letting the worst of me
Get the best.

When I tell him, "Come on, Steinie. Let's go, boy,"
He shakes off however much of whatever
Hasn't fallen on us just now.

LINES

WRITTEN DURING A RECENT SYMPOSIUM ON THE "DEATH OF POETRY"

My guess is, the gods don't give
A damn. I don't even think
They can tell us apart.

They probably see
All of us hopping
From reading to reading like robins

Common on a morning's wet lawn,
Our pin-feathered heads pivoting
This way and that, as though

Listening for the gods
Themselves in the ground.
Can't you hear them laughing?

—What lunatic peckers! they roar.

—What worms! come back the robins.

THE RICH MAN FINDS THE WIDOWER ALONE

I find him out walking,
And when I ask him how he feels,

He doesn't know
What to say.

Lowering his head, he goes on, hands sounding out
One another like sparrows on the gravel.

It's coming back to him now, those nights
She ghosted the bed beside him

And he lay there wondering where the sounds she made in
                                        dreams
Came from,

Sounds that used to
Ease him down to sleep

But these nights needle him awake—
Notes so slowed

Their melody is
Just now beginning to be heard under

The rending each made
Coming into being.

A WALK LATE ON THE WORLD'S FAIR SITE

Moonlight? Who can say?
All I recall
Are your eyes
In the streetlamps ringing

A carp pond in back of the pavilion.
I thought I had lost you
Through stupidity,
And nothing calmed me,

Nor that ache for something
Nothing else can ease,
Though I looked everywhere.
That's when I heard, or thought

I heard, you call my name.
It had never before
Sounded
On the wind like that,

So likewise
Filled with longing—
When I looked back,
There was nothing

But you among the blossoms'
Four petalled pearling,
Scented and brighter and gone
Into the company of others.

FIRST MUSIC

By the time we wheel the mower and edger
To the garage,
Fireflies are testing the undersea green bulbs of early evening—

There's no more denying them
Than there is
Getting around whatever it is *we* brim with, and sway to,
                                        sock-footed in jeans, in a kitchen
That looms as night comes on.

It's the same I remember one night feeling cooling in the waste
                                                        dunes
Of southern California
Watching a scorpion drag
One of its paralyzed own down.

—Not that very moment,
But the next,
When they moved off as one.

FOG SHARKS

In the great valley of those nights
No one could account for
The waywardness of what

Sometimes happened—
The tule-needled sloughs simmering
So much mist it took two to drive—

One to steer and one to walk ahead—
Fog sharks, we'd say, and laugh.
Fog sharks, we'd say, and shrug.

—Odd to figure all that water
In the desert stretch the valley
Once was—flowerings that couldn't

Live at all, let alone
Summer under the sun of central California
Until the honeydews drew only

Bees and ants, and the corn stalks
And cotton trees towered
Over workers in the field.

—Standing on that heat-willowing
Sand back then, all that snow
Simmering on the western Sierra Nevadas,

And nothing between you and it
And flash-flooding followed by drought
But your mind backing the fat rivers

Into channels wide as highways
Bearing the deep waters on,
Some with catfish six feet long.

ITS DIFFICULT NAME

From California my sister
Four years ago called

To say two feet
Of rain had

Fallen during morning on
The desert place she and I once survived.

She said,
Would you believe it?—

My wooden ducks, in the yard,
The ducks are floating away.

She said, I don't even know
What it means he said I've got.

So I went to the medical journals,
And the growth rates, and charts,

And I learned in the living roots
Of a dead language

Its difficult name,
And I said it

Until it lost all meaning
And its sound drifted off

Like anything else breeze-borne
Over the soils and waters of the earth.

These days, I find
Its echo everywhere—

There, and here, and now—
As when, one year of her death today,

I sound it again, inwardly, to myself,

And its meaning has no language, still,
And does not

Come back at all.

BODY AND SOUL

It's just that
Slightly crazy.

One way
Of looking at it is,
How can I *not*
Think of it?

Another is,
How *can* I?

I don't know what to call
The color of the dog's bowl,
Though gold in the light
It settles on,
It could be dust.

Every time I look at it,
The dead dog drinks.
Every time I walk away,
It thirsts.

SUMMER'S REPUBLIC

Every year, this foolishness
Of palmetto fronds
And sea fresh breezes

Rumor-salted
That the world of matter
Is immune to time.

At least it feels
That way watching
One young thing walking

An early morning island's
High-tide
Whisper of a beach

To its rocky point.
For a while after
She is gone, there seems

Nothing to replace
The bright republic she was.
Though soon, umbrellas

And clown-colored towels
Claim the newly soothed sand,
And other girls up

The shore and back
Walk the lemon-scented
Limbs

They have found just
This morning
Forced in the windy sun—

TO A MONARCH DROWNED IN THE ATLANTIC

She and I made sweet breakfast
Of one of the low-country cantaloupes,
And from the seaside villa
Hurried south
Over the two miles of beach
The lowering tide widened,
Almost to the island's end.

A sandbar surfaces there, briefly,
And fans that blond light as far away east
As you can see.

Looking at it, it's simple
To think you could wade across
That murky, four- and five-feet deep trough,
And keep walking on that sand
For a morning, or a century,
Or until you tired
Or missed someone so badly you had to walk forever on
Or face your own steps back
Before the sea slipped between.

It's always simpler
To think so—

And then I saw you,
So recently dead
Your rich wings held their own against the sea.

I stood there, knowing
Even if I called
And she took her quick steps

Returning from where she had wandered away,
It would have been too late, the sea already sweeping up.

I stayed as long as I could,
And by the time she waved back over
All that breathing sand
To where some semblance of me stood,
The sea's winds had swept us away
Cleaner than I could have imagined,
And washed us up here, in whatever radiance
We have been reduced to.

THE BRILLIANT DAYS

Bright for you shone the days,
    I remember a man singing
        a long time ago, his inheritance

Of a meager life run through
    by thirty. I'm over fifty and cold
        to my knees in a river

Of actuality he never lived
    and traveled long enough to see.
        I'm out here watching

Bright carvings of the sun
    on the watery burden ease
        their slow time toward me,

A few ripples molten, my good mind
    on the sleek river rocks
        in front of me—shining and in shadow,

Swimming and sinking at once—
    and the long weeds trailing from them,
        goodbye, goodbye.

When I turn around and look,
    they are still waving, though now
        they are pulling away.

PAYING FOR WHAT YOU GET

My father liked
To say by summing up
That you get
What you pay for.

I see that as the wisdom of a man
Who has been used.

I wouldn't have believed you, either,
If you hadn't been kind enough
To drive me there,
But one summer I discovered
That some sand dollars
Have a coarse purple fur on them
Freshly washed-up,
Because I happened to come across some
That had been freshly washed-up
With a coarse fur on them
That was purple.

In the light,
When the morning's made lighter
By water and sand,
You can see the hairs can be brushed back and forth
Like velour beginning to stiffen,
And after a few days
On a balcony
Breeze-heated and sand-dusted,
The color of its life
Bleaches back out
Into the light you are taking in
And the air through which
It both ways moves.

From the cloud-colored disk
The cilia themselves
Seem to have fallen away,
And while you're peering as closely as you can,
Trying to see along
The bottom of the thing, the body
Crumbles itself in your hands
To sand again.

Unless someone has brought you here,
You would never believe
That the wind from the warm sea—while you watch—
Spirits even that away.